SEATTLE
Where Coffee Reigns

Emerald Point Press ®

▲

"*Seattle* — it may not always rain,
But the coffee always pours."

SEATTLE
WHERE COFFEE REIGNS

Editor
GREG SAFFELL

Text
ERICA BAUERMEISTER

Photography
CHRIS JACOBSON

ISBN 0-9637816-9-3

COPYRIGHT©2004
EMERALD POINT PRESS®
SEATTLE, WASHINGTON
www.emeraldpointpress.com

PRINTED IN CHINA

*I*t's a cool, grey Seattle morning, and the rain is falling softly but persistently. The days are short in the winter, and a car's lights can be on more often than not. Luckily, the line to the counter is short as well, and it doesn't take long before your hands touch the slick surface of a white, ceramic cup, and warmth steams up towards your face. The first sip finds its way to your stomach, and suddenly you are a cat in the windowsill, a child cuddled in a down quilt. And awake. What a combination.

If nature gave Seattle rain, man gave it espresso. When you see the sheer number of coffee houses in Seattle, staking their claim to every corner, shoe-horned into bookstores and gas stations, it might be tempting to think coffee was born here, but the origins are far, far more remote than that. Popular legend traces the discovery of coffee beans back to an Ethiopian goat herder named Kaldi who, sometime around 850A.D., noticed his goats cavorting about a particular shrub, eating its berries. The goats were so invigorated, in fact, that sleeping proved difficult. Kaldi told the local monks, who became intrigued with the implications for those who had difficulty staying awake through evening prayers.

The drink made from the crushed beans boiled in water proved highly successful — and popular, quickly moving beyond the confines of the local mosques and into public coffee houses. In countries where the local religion forbid alcohol and the water was often unpalatable, coffee provided a stimulating and attractive alternative, particularly when combined with coffee houses that included conversation and music. By 1475, twenty cups a day was not unusual among the upper classes and Turkish law even allowed a woman to divorce her husband if he failed to keep the coffee pot supplied.

The spread of coffee throughout the rest of the world is a story of intrigue, romance, power, and the ever-present challenge of climate. For while the warming and invigorating qualities of coffee made it an almost immediate success in cold, wet Europe, propagation of the plant in those regions proved almost as impossible as getting seeds or plants past their Middle Eastern distributors, who were careful to make sure any exported beans were partially boiled or roasted. Around 1600, an intrepid Moslem pilgrim named Baba Budan managed to smuggle out seven seeds by taping them to his stomach, and planted the seeds in southern India. In 1616, the Dutch got a tree and started growing coffee in Ceylon. King Louis XIV of France, himself besotted with the beverage, finally obtained a tree through the Dutch in 1714 and grew it in a special greenhouse.

And then, things got exciting. In 1723, a young French naval officer named Gabriel de Clieu stole several seedlings from King Louis XIV's tree (with, or perhaps not, the aid of an enamored insider) and set off for Martinique where he hoped the climate would prove more favorable than a Paris greenhouse. The journey was difficult — there were jealous fellow travelers to contend with, storms at sea, periods of calm so long that de Clieu finally resorted to sharing his own water rations with his precious cargo. By the time he arrived, de Clieu had only one of his precious treasures remaining – but within fifty years, that resilient seedling had multiplied into over eighteen million coffee plants.

Only four years after de Clieu's voyage, another young man grasped an opportunity. Francesco Melo Palhetta, a Portuguese Brazilian, was sent to mediate a boundary dispute between French and Dutch Guiana. The dispute was settled, and when young Palhetta left, it was with a bouquet from the French governor's wife. In it were hidden coffee seeds — from which

Brazil's current giant coffee industry grew.

By 1750, coffee was being grown on five continents. By 1999, it was second only to oil as the most valuable exported (legal) commodity in the world. It is estimated that production and sale of coffee employ over twenty million people – a long way from Kaldi and his dancing herd.

For almost as long as there has been coffee, there have been coffeehouses. Perhaps it is the stimulating nature of coffee, bringing on the desire for conversation and interaction. Perhaps it is simply a human desire to meet, tell stories, make connections. But wherever coffee has traveled, gathering places have not been far behind, from the *qahveh khaneh* of Mecca to the cafés of Paris and Vienna, and the espresso bars of Italy.

Oddly enough, it was in England where coffeehouses made their initial mark outside of the Middle East. The first was opened in Oxford in 1650; by 1700, there were over 2,000 in the city of London alone. Coffee houses had their own sets of rules, newsletters, and self-selected clientele. They were called "penny universities" because for the price of a cup of coffee, you could join or listen in on hours of stimulating conversation.

Not everyone loved the British coffeehouses, however. Unlike their counterparts in France or Italy, where men and women mingled equally, London coffeehouses were the province of men. Whether the Women's Petition Against Coffee was prompted by the exclusionary nature of coffeehouses or a real concern about the effects of coffee will never be completely ascertained, but its publication, along with a concern that coffeehouses were "the great resort of idle and disaffected persons," caused King Charles II to proclaim a ban on coffeehouses in 1675. Not that it worked — the uproar was so great that two days before the ban was

due to go into effect, King Charles backed down. By 1715, London had the highest consumption of coffee of any city in the world.

In the end, it was not women or Charles II who changed England's beverage of choice from coffee to tea, but the East India Company, which saw a greater profit in leaves than beans. Some of the original coffeehouses still remain, however, although in interestingly altered forms. Edward Lloyd's coffeehouse, which regularly posted ships' lists for insurers, is now Lloyd's of London. Jonathan's, a favorite hangout of London financiers, became the London Stock Exchange, while other coffeehouses turned into the headquarters for The Spectator and The Tattler.

But wherever coffeehouses have existed, artists and rebels have found them. Around the tables of Café Procope — the first café opened in Paris — Robespierre, Danton and Marat planned revolt against Louis XVI and Marie Antoinette. Voltaire was known to drink as many as forty cups of mocha a day, preferring to mix his coffee with chocolate. Legend has it that Napoleon Bonaparte, who mixed coffee with chess instead, left behind his three-cornered hat as a claim against unpaid bills. In the new world of the not-yet United States, the Green Dragon of Boston provided a meeting place for Paul Revere and Samuel Adams to plot a revolution; it was at the Merchant's Coffee House in Philadelphia that the Declaration of Independence was read aloud to the public for the first time. Some two hundred years later, on the other side of the country, Allen Ginsberg, Jack Kerouac and Lawrence Ferlinghetti found literary havens at the Coffee Gallery and the Co-Existence Bagel Shop of San Francisco.

During those two hundred years between Paul Revere's ride and the Beat Generation, Americans adopted coffee as their drink of choice. From the moment of the Boston Tea Party, it became a patriotic act to choose beans over leaves and by 1940 the United States was importing seventy percent of the world's coffee crop.

Unfortunately, while countries such as France and Italy were developing espresso machines and recipes for elegant small and large cups of strong or foaming beverages, America went the way of percolators and instant coffee. A small but determined faction, including Alfred Peet of Berkeley, California, began promoting other alternatives, but it took Howard Schultz of Starbucks, drawing on his experiences with espresso bars while traveling in Italy, to make espresso an American institution. From its initial store in Seattle's Pike Place Market, Starbucks has turned into a marketing force, with more than 7,000 stores worldwide and over 80 in Seattle alone. Bringing the story full circle, Peet's Coffee opened their first store in Seattle in the summer of 2003. Along

THE ORIGINAL STARBUCKS IN THE PIKE PLACE PUBLIC MARKET, SEATTLE

the way, Seattle has become synonymous with coffee—with the daily ritual of lattes, cappuccinos and even Americanos weaving itself into the fabric of the urban Seattle lifestyle.

While you might think all that coffee would make for some jittery citizens, in general, espresso has less caffeine – one-half to one-third – than canned coffee made from cheaper coffee beans. Not to mention that the process of making espresso one cup at a time requires a certain amount of patience and finesse. Whether you drink your espresso straight from a tiny white cup, or out of a wide, bowl-shaped tureen with steamed milk and a heart or a feather design gracing the surface, espresso begs for pause and reflection — and, often, a little something to eat. While the old American coffee cried out for donuts, the new American espresso, with all its European overtones, opens the cultural door to croissants and scones, brioche and biscotti. And with better, more flavorful beans comes the prospect of coffee-flavored mousse or cheesecake, or perhaps an espresso torte…

EARLY MORNING, SEATTLE'S BEST COFFEE, PIKE PLACE PUBLIC MARKET

The options seem endless. But what could be better than a luscious chocolate mocha truffle cake, warm from the oven, accompanied by a bracing macchiato or a tall and soothing latte. Who knows – a little coffee here, a little cookery there – you just might make it through that long, Seattle winter…

The menu board reads:

Raspberry ...
Blueberry Bran
Lemon Poppy Seed
Cranberry Almond

Croissants
Plain   Chocolate
Almond   Raspberry
Savory Spinach Feta

Scones
Wild Blueberry
Pumpkin Spice
Peach Passionfruit
Orange Currant
Mixed Berry Multigrain
Strawberry

Breads
Lemon Pound
Banana Walnut

Coffeecake
Brioche

HOLLY'S ON QUEEN ANNE, SEATTLE

16

Coffee Drink Dictionary

Ordering Yours from the Barista.

Caffè Latte – Espresso with steamed milk and in some instances a small cap of foam.

Caffè Mocha – A latte with chocolate syrup or powder added.

Cappuccino – A shot of espresso with the rest being half steamed and half milk foam.

Café Au Lait – Coffee and heated milk poured simultaneously.

Caffè Americano – Espresso diluted with an equal portion of hot water.

Breve – Espresso with steamed half-and-half or cream.

Espresso – A one to two ounce drink made by forcing hot water under pressure through finely ground coffee beans.

Caffè Freddo – Iced coffee.

Doppio – A double shot of espresso.

Granita – A latte made with a sweetened frozen milk mixture.

This is a basic list of definitions. Many places have specialty drinks that can be quite interesting. Review the menu and ask questions.

The Recipes

Coffee is an experience in itself. We have come a long way since the days of a common cup of Joe. With the variety of beans and roasts available, blends are endless. While trying them all might be an impossible task, finding a taste that pleases you is not difficult. Experiment with different coffee drinks. Ask your next barista to prepare one of his or her favorites. Like wine, multiple tastings educate your palate, helping you to determine what's best for you. You can enjoy coffee by itself or couple it with a tasty treat. The recipes that follow may enhance your coffee drinking experience. I have my favorites, and I invite you to discover yours! Enjoying good friends, good coffee and sweet delicious desserts, is enjoying life.

iscotti

3 cups flour

2 1/2 teaspoons baking powder

1 cup sugar

1/2 teaspoon salt

1/2 cup slightly toasted almonds, chopped

3 large eggs, beaten

1/2 cup butter, melted and cooled

1 teaspoon vanilla

1 teaspoon almond extract

2 tablespoons anise seed

Preheat oven to 350 degrees.

Grease two baking sheets. In a large mixing bowl, combine flour, baking powder, sugar and salt; set aside. In a separate bowl, combine beaten eggs with melted butter, almonds, anise seeds, vanilla and almond extracts.

Make a well in the center of the flour mixture and stir in the egg mixture. Turn out onto a lightly floured board and knead until smooth. Shape dough into four long rolls, each about as wide as your thumb and arrange several inches apart on the greased cookie sheets. Bake 20 minutes, or until rolls are golden brown and slightly flattened.

Transfer cookie rolls to cooling rack and cool 10 minutes. Slice each roll on a long diagonal into 1/2-inch slices and return slices to cookie sheets. Bake 10 minutes, or until slightly brown, then turn each cookie over and bake 10 minutes longer.

Cool cookies on racks and store tightly covered.

Makes 2 1/2 dozen large cookies

Bittersweet Fudge Sauce

In a heavy saucepan, stir cocoa, sugars, and salt until blended.

Mix in the cream and butter. Heat, stirring constantly, to boiling.

Let stand for 5 minutes. Stir in vanilla. Serve warm over ice cream.

1 cup Dutch cocoa

3/4 cup sugar

1/2 cup brown sugar

Pinch of salt

3/4 cup heavy cream

4 ounces (1 stick) unsalted butter

1 teaspoon vanilla

Makes 2 cups

$\mathscr{B}$rownies

Preheat oven to 350 degrees.

Grease and flour a 9 x 12 inch baking pan.

Melt butter and chocolate in the top part of a double boiler over boiling water. When melted, set aside to cool to room temperature.

Meanwhile, beat eggs and sugar until thick and lemon-colored, add vanilla. Fold chocolate mixture into eggs and sugar. Mix thoroughly.

Sift flour and fold gently into batter, mixing just until blended. Fold in walnuts.

Pour into prepared pan. Bake for 25 minutes, or until center is just set. Do not overbake.

Allow brownies to cool in pan for 30 minutes before cutting into bars.

1/2 pound (2 sticks) butter

4 ounces unsweetened chocolate

2 cups sugar

1/2 cup flour

2/3 cup walnuts, coarsely chopped

4 eggs

1 teaspoon vanilla

Makes 28 large brownies

Black-Bottom Cupcakes

CUPCAKES

3 cups all purpose flour

2 cups sugar

1/2 cup cocoa

2 teaspoons baking soda

1/2 teaspoon salt

2 cups water

5 ounces oil

2 tablespoons white vinegar

2 teaspoons vanilla

FILLING

3 tablespoons sugar

6 ounces chocolate chips

8 ounces cream cheese

1 egg

Preheat oven to 350 degrees.

CUPCAKES

This batter can be made in one bowl with a simple whisk. Put dry ingredients in a large bowl. Add liquid ingredients to dry mixture. Whisk until smooth. Fill lined cupcake pan 3/4 full with batter.

FILLING

Blend together the cream cheese, sugar, and egg in separate bowl. Add chocolate chips and mix.

Put one spoonful of filling on top of cupcake batter.
Bake for 20-25 minutes until firm.

Makes 24

Buttermilk Chocolate Cake

Have all ingredients at room temperature. Preheat the oven to 350 degrees and adjust the rack to the lower third of the oven. Grease and flour two 9-inch cake pans. Sift together the flour, baking soda and salt; set aside.

Using a mixer cream the butter until smooth. Add the sugar and continue to cream until light and fluffy. Add the eggs, one at a time, beating well after each addition. Beat in the vanilla, then the cooled melted chocolate.

Add the dry ingredients alternately with the buttermilk, beginning and ending with the dry ingredients. Divide the batter equally between the two pans, spreading to level the tops. Bake for approximately 24 minutes or until a wooden toothpick, inserted into the center of the cakes, comes out clean. Cool in the pans on a wire rack for 10 to 15 minutes. Invert and remove pans. Cool completely on racks before frosting.

FROSTING

Cream together the sugar, salt and butter. Slowly add the buttermilk, mixing until smooth. Blend in the cooled melted chocolate and vanilla. Add additional powdered sugar if the frosting seems too runny or a little more buttermilk if too thick, to achieve a smooth consistency.

Spread the frosting between the layers, around the sides and top of the cake.

2 cups cake flour

1/4 teaspoon salt

1 teaspoon baking soda

1/2 cup unsalted butter, softened

1 cup sugar

2 eggs

1 teaspoon vanilla

1 cup buttermilk

2 ounces unsweetened chocolate, melted and cooled

BUTTERMILK CHOCOLATE FROSTING

2 cups powdered sugar

1/8 teaspoon salt

3 tablespoons buttermilk

2 tablespoons unsalted butter, softened

4 ounces unsweetened chocolate, melted

1 teaspoon vanilla

Carole's Carrot Cake with Cream Cheese Frosting

Preheat oven to 350 degrees.

Into a large bowl, sift together flour, baking powder, baking soda, salt and cinnamon and stir in sugar, oil, eggs, carrot, pineapple, coconut, and walnuts.

Divide the batter between 2 buttered and floured 9-inch round cake pans, and bake the layers in the middle of the oven for 35-40 minutes, or until a tester comes out clean. Let the layers cool in the pans on a rack for 5 minutes; run a thin knife around the edge of each pan, and invert the layers onto the rack to cool completely.

FROSTING

In a bowl with an electric mixer, beat together the cream cheese, butter, and vanilla until the mixture is fluffy; add the confectioners' sugar gradually, beating until the frosting is smooth.

Arrange one of the cake layers, bottom side up on a cake plate and spread the top with some of the frosting. Put the remaining cake layer, bottom side up on the frosting and spread the remaining frosting over the top and side of the cake.

2 cups all-purpose flour

2 teaspoons double-acting baking powder

1 1/2 teaspoons baking soda

1 1/2 teaspoons salt

2 teaspoons cinnamon

2 cups sugar

1 1/3 cups confectioners' sugar

1/2 cup chopped walnuts

1 1/2 cups vegetable oil

4 large eggs

8 ounces cream cheese, softened

1 stick (1/2cup) unsalted butter, softened

1 teaspoon vanilla

2 cups finely grated peeled carrot

8 ounce can crushed pineapple, drained

1 cup sweetened flaked coconut

Caramel Crunch Cake

CAKE

1 1/4 cups sifted cake flour

1 1/2 cups sugar

1 teaspoon salt

6 egg yolks

7 egg whites

1/4 cup water

1 tablespoon lemon juice

1 teaspoon vanilla

1 teaspoon cream of tartar

TOPPING

1 1/2 cups sugar

3 teaspoons baking soda

2 tablespoons powdered sugar

1/4 cup light corn syrup

1 cup heavy cream

1 teaspoon vanilla

1/4 cup strong coffee

Preheat oven to 350 degrees.

Mix together the flour, 3/4 cup of the sugar, egg yolks, water, lemon juice, and vanilla. Beat until a smooth batter is formed.

Whip the egg whites with the cream of tartar and salt until soft peaks form. Beat in the remaining 3/4 cup of sugar, a tablespoon at a time, until the egg whites are stiff. Gently fold the batter into the whites until just blended. Spoon into an ungreased tube pan. Bake for 50-55 minutes, or until the top springs back when touched. Remove from the oven and immediately invert over the neck of a bottle. Let the cake hang until cool. Loosen with a knife and remove from the pan.

TOPPING

Combine the sugar, coffee and syrup in a saucepan. Stir and bring to a boil. Cook until it reaches 310 degrees on a candy thermometer. Remove from the heat and immediately add the soda. Stir vigorously just until the topping thickens and pulls away from the sides of the pan. Immediately pour into an ungreased shallow metal pan. Do not stir or spread. Let cool. When cool, knock out of pan. Crush into coarse crumbs.

Slice the cake into 4 layers. Whip the heavy cream with the powdered sugar and vanilla until firm. Spread half of the whipped cream between layers. Spread the remainder on the top and sides of the cake. Refrigerate until ready to serve. Just prior to serving, cover the cake generously with the crushed caramel topping.

Serves 8-10

Cat's Tongue Cookies

In a medium bowl, sift together the flour, sugar and ginger.

In a bowl, beat the egg white with an electric mixer until the mixture mounds slightly, about 1 minute. Do not overbeat to soft peaks.

In a medium bowl, beat the cream on high speed until it thickens but does not hold its shape, about 30 to 60 seconds. Fold the beaten egg white into the cream, then add to the flour mixture and stir until well blended. Cover and set aside until the batter thickens to the consistency of molasses, 10 to 15 minutes.

Preheat the oven to 400 degrees. Brush some of the melted butter over a baking sheet. Dip the blade of a dinner knife into the batter and scoop up about 1 teaspoon. Tap the batter-coated blade on the cookie sheet and draw the knife down about 2 1/2inches to form a thin line of batter. Continue forming cookies in this manner, leaving about 2 inches in between them, until the sheet is filled.

Bake the cookies in the middle of the oven for 4 to 5 minutes, until the edges are lightly browned. Let the cookies cool on the sheet for 2 minutes, then remove with a metal spatula and place on a wire rack to cool. (If the cookies harden on the sheet, rewarm briefly in the oven.) Wipe the cookie sheet clean and brush again with melted butter. Continue shaping and baking the cookies in this manner until all of the batter is used.

1/3 cup flour

2/3 cup confectioners sugar

1 teaspoon powdered ginger

1 egg white

1/4 cup heavy cream

2 tablespoons unsalted butter, melted

Makes about 4 dozen cookies

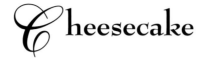heesecake

3 tablespoons brown
  sugar

1 cup plus 2 tablespoons
  sugar

1 1/2 cups ground
  almonds

1/3 cup butter, more for
  pan

1 1/2 pounds cream
  cheese, softened

1 pint sour cream

4 egg whites

1 tablespoon plus 1/4
  teaspoon vanilla

Preheat oven to 350 degrees.

In a small bowl, combine almonds and brown sugar. Melt butter, then stir in. Butter bottom and sides of a 9-inch springform pan, then press nut mixture into bottom but not up sides.

In a small pan, warm cream cheese over low heat. When very soft, remove from heat, and set aside. In a large bowl, whisk egg whites and 1 cup sugar until they hold soft peaks. Fold in cream cheese and 1 tablespoon vanilla. Pour into pan, and bake 25-30 minutes, until a toothpick inserted in center comes out only slightly moist; cake should not be brown.

Meanwhile, in a small bowl, whisk together sour cream, remaining sugar and vanilla. When cake comes out of oven, increase setting to 450 degrees, and carefully spread mixture over cake. Return it to oven for 5 minutes. Do not overcook or it will crack or turn brown. Remove, and let cool in pan. Chill in refrigerator.

To serve, run a knife along edge of pan, and remove sides of pan. Cut into wedges and serve.

Serves 8

Cherry Scones

Soak cherries in apple or grape juice at least 10 minutes. Drain well.

In a processor or bowl, mix flour, 1/4 cup of sugar, baking powder, soda, nutmeg and salt. Add butter and process or cut in with pastry blender until mixture has fine crumbs. Stir in egg, yogurt, peel and cherries.

Turn dough out on lightly oiled 12-by-15-inch baking sheet. Lightly flour hands and pat dough into 9-inch round. With a knife, cut into 8 pie-shaped wedges. Sprinkle with remaining 1/4 cup of sugar.

Bake in an oven preheated to 375 degrees until golden brown and firm to the touch, about 20 minutes. Serve warm with butter and/or orange marmalade.

2 cups flour

1/2 cup sugar (divided)

2 teaspoons baking powder

1/2 teaspoon baking soda

1/2 teaspoon fresh ground nutmeg

1/2 teaspoon salt

1/2 cup dried cherries

apple or grape juice (enough to cover cherries)

1/4 cup cold butter, cut into 1/2 inch cubes

1 egg

1/2 cup plain yogurt

1 teaspoon lemon or orange peel

Makes 8

Chocolate Chip Coffee Cake

TOPPING

1/4 cup sugar

1/3 cup brown sugar

1 teaspoon cinnamon

1 cup chopped nuts

1 cup chocolate chips

CAKE

1 cup sugar

1 teaspoon baking powder

1 teaspoon baking soda

1 teaspoon salt

2 cups sifted flour

4 ounces unsalted butter, softened

2 eggs

1 cup sour cream

2 teaspoons vanilla

TOPPING

Combine all of the ingredients. Mix well and set aside.

CAKE

Preheat oven to 350 degrees. Cream the butter and sugar until smooth. Add the eggs, sour cream, vanilla, baking powder, baking soda and salt. Mix well. Stir in flour and mix until just blended. Generously butter a tube pan. Sprinkle with half of topping. Spoon half of the batter over topping. With a knife, gently swirl topping and batter together. Spread with the remaining topping. Cover with the remaining batter. Bake for 45 to 50 minutes, or until a tester inserted in the center comes out clean.

Serves 8

Chocolate Chip Cookies

Preheat oven to 375 degrees.

In a bowl, cream butter and sugars; add egg and vanilla.
In a separate bowl, mix together flour, oatmeal, salt, baking
powder and baking soda. Combine wet and dry ingredients,
add chocolate chips, grated chocolate and nuts.

Make golf ball-sized cookies and bake on ungreased cookie sheet
2 inches apart, for 6-10 minutes. Do not overbake.

1 cup flour

1/3 cup sugar

1/3 cup brown sugar

**1 1/4 cup oatmeal (mix
in blender until it turns
to powder; measure
first then blend)**

1/4 teaspoon salt

**1/2 teaspoon baking
powder**

**1/2 teaspoon baking
soda**

**1 (6-oz) bag chocolate
chips**

**2 ounces milk chocolate,
grated**

1/2 cup butter

1 egg

1/2 teaspoon vanilla

Makes about 2 dozen cookies

Chocolate Espresso Beans

Preheat oven to 350 degrees.

Place the espresso beans on a baking sheet and toast for 8-10 minutes (or use pre-roasted beans instead). Let cool. Melt the chocolate in a double boiler over barely simmering water until smooth and creamy. Drop in the espresso beans and stir until the beans are coated. Remove the beans with a slotted spoon and allow the excess chocolate to drip off. Place the beans on waxed paper, separating them so they do not stick together.

When the coated beans are cool but the chocolate is still pliable, roll the beans in your hands to form round balls. Roll each ball in cocoa and set aside until the chocolate coating has set completely.

1 cup espresso beans

3 tablespoons cocoa

4 ounces milk chocolate

Makes about 1 1/2 cups

Chocolate Espresso Torte

1 cup sugar

2 tablespoons espresso beans

2 tablespoons hazelnuts or almonds

1 cup unsalted butter

9 eggs, separated

1/4 cup brewed espresso

16 ounces semisweet chocolate

Sifted powdered sugar or cocoa for dusting

Preheat oven to 350 degrees. Butter a 10-inch springform pan. Line the bottom with buttered waxed paper and dust the pan with cocoa or finely ground espresso. Place the nuts and espresso beans in separate shallow baking pans and place them in the oven for 8-10 minutes, or until lightly toasted. If using hazelnuts, wrap them in a clean dish towel and let cool, then rub them between the cloth and your hands to remove the dark brown skins. Grind the nuts in a blender or food processor, and finely grind the espresso beans in a coffee grinder.

In a heavy saucepan over very low heat, melt the chocolate and butter together. Stir in the ground espresso beans and nuts: pour into a bowl to cool. In a large bowl, beat the yolks for about 1 minute. Slowly add the sugar and continue beating until thick and pale. Add the brewed espresso to the yolk mixture, then add the cooled chocolate mixture and blend thoroughly.

In another large bowl, beat the egg whites until soft peaks form. Pour the chocolate and yolk mixture into the egg whites and fold gently until completely blended. Pour the batter into the prepared pan and bake for 40-45 minutes, or until the edges begin to pull away from the sides of the pan.

Let the torte cool on the rack for 30 minutes. Run a knife around the edges of the cake to loosen it, then remove the sides of the pan. Run a long narrow knife under the bottom of the pan. Invert the torte, remove the paper, and place the torte on a serving plate. Dust with powdered sugar or cocoa to serve.

Chocolate Espresso Truffles

Place the chocolate chips in a heat-proof bowl and set aside.

In a small saucepan, whisk together the cream, sugar, corn syrup and espresso powder. Place over medium heat and bring the mixture just to a boil. Pour this cream mixture into the bowl containing the chocolate chips, making sure the chips are completely covered. Allow the mixture to stand a few minutes. As soon as the chocolate begins to melt, slowly start whisking the mixture, gently blending the cream into the melted chocolate. When the chocolate and cream are completely smooth, gradually begin to add the butter - a few pieces at a time - whisking constantly until all of the butter has been added. Allow the mixture to chill in the refrigerator until firm enough to scoop.

Lightly coat the bottom of a shallow container with a few teaspoons of the cocoa powder. Use a small scoop to scoop the truffles, placing them in the container. Allow the truffles to chill until they are firm enough to handle, then roll each truffle between your hands to form a smooth round ball — then placing it in a bowl with the remaing cocoa powder.

Continue rolling the remaining truffles, tossing them with the cocoa powder to completely coat them as you work.

1/2 cup sugar

2 tablespoons instant espresso powder

1 cup (approx.) cocoa powder

1 1/8 cups bittersweet chocolate chips

1 cup milk chocolate chips

1/2 cup heavy cream

2 tablespoons light corn syrup

2 sticks unsalted butter, softened, cut into small pieces

Makes about 30-40

Chocolate Madeleines

1/2 cup cake flour

2 teaspoons cocoa

1/2 teaspoon baking powder

4 tablespoons sugar

4 ounces (1 stick) unsalted butter

2 eggs

1 teaspoon vanilla

1 teaspoon hot water

1/2 teaspoon brandy

2 ounces semisweet chocolate

Butter for molds

Powdered sugar

Preheat oven to 325 degrees. Brush Madeleine molds with the butter. Melt the chocolate with the butter. Beat the eggs with the sugar until thick. Beat in the chocolate mixture, vanilla, hot water, and brandy. Add the flour, cocoa, and baking powder. Mix just until the flour in the mixture disappears. Spoon the batter into the prepared molds, filling 2/3 full. Bake for 10-12 minutes or until a tester inserted in the center is clean. Loosen the Madeleines and invert the pan over a cake rack. Cool to room temperature. Dust with powdered sugar before serving.

Makes 18-20 cookies

Chocolate Raspberry Cake

CAKE

Preheat oven to 400 degrees. Line an 8-inch cake pan with parchment paper. In a saucepan, melt the chocolate and butter over low heat. Place uncracked eggs in a bowl of hot water for 5 minutes. Crack and combine the eggs and sugar in the bowl of an electric mixer. Beat on high speed for 8-10 minutes, or until tripled in volume. Sift the flour on top. Fold into the eggs. Stir 1/4 of the egg mixture into the chocolate. Carefully fold the chocolate into the remaining eggs until thoroughly combined.

Pour into the prepared pan. Bake for 20 minutes. The cake will still be slightly soft in the middle. Cool completely in the pan. Cover and refrigerate in the pan overnight. The cake can be frozen for two weeks at this point.

RASPBERRY SAUCE

Puree the raspberries and strain. Add enough sugar to sweeten. Whip the heavy cream with the vanilla until firm. Invert the cake onto a platter and cut into wedges. Spoon some of the raspberry sauce onto the bottom of a dessert plate. Place a wedge of the cake in the center of the sauce. Spoon a dollop of whipped cream on top of the cake. Form a circle with raspberries around the wedge.

CAKE

1 tablespoon flour

1 tablespoon sugar

1 pound sweet chocolate

4 eggs

6 ounces (1 1/2 sticks) unsalted butter

RASPBERRY SAUCE

8 ounces raspberries, fresh or frozen

Superfine sugar to taste

1 cup heavy cream

1 teaspoon vanilla

Fresh raspberries

Serves 8-10

hocolate Souffle

5 tablespoons sugar, plus additional for dusting soufflé dish

4 ounces semisweet chocolate, coarsely chopped

Confectioners' sugar

3 tablespoons milk

2 egg yolks

3 egg whites

Preheat oven to 375 degrees.

Place milk and 4 tablespoons sugar in a small saucepan and stir over a medium-low heat until sugar dissolves — about 45 seconds. Stir in chocolate and cook until melted — 1-2 minutes. Transfer to a non-reactive bowl (glass or stainless steel), cool for 5 minutes, then beat in egg yolks.

Beat egg whites in a non-reactive bowl until foamy, then sprinkle in remaining sugar, beating until stiff peaks form.

Butter a small soufflé dish (2 1/2 inches deep; 6-inch diameter; soufflé will not rise in a large dish), and then lightly dust with sugar. Gently mix one-third of the egg whites into chocolate mixture, and then fold in remaining whites, one-third at a time. Do not over-mix. Spoon batter into dish.

Make sure oven rack is low enough to allow soufflé room to rise as much as 2 inches above the dish. Bake until puffed, about 25 minutes. Dust with confectioners' sugar and serve immediately (soufflé will begin to deflate after about 2 minutes).

Serves 3-4

innamon Stars

Preheat oven to 350 degrees.

Sift flour, cinnamon, and salt together onto a sheet of waxed paper.

In a large mixing bowl, cream butter and brown sugar together until light and fluffy. Add egg yolk and beat until light. Add flour mixture and blend well. Cover and chill cookie dough in refrigerator for at least 1 hour or overnight.

Divide dough in half. On a lightly floured surface, roll out half of dough 1/8 inch thick. Using a 2 1/2 inch star-shaped cookie cutter, cut out cookies and place them 2 inches apart on a lightly greased baking sheet. Roll and cut out second half of dough and arrange on baking sheet. Sprinkle cookies with granulated sugar.

Bake in the center of hot oven for 7 to 8 minutes, or until firm and just beginning to brown around the edges. Transfer to a wire rack and let cool. Store in a tightly covered container.

1 cup flour

1 1/2 teaspoons ground cinnamon

Pinch of salt

1/2 cup firmly packed light brown sugar

2 tablespoons sugar

1/2 cup (1 stick) unsalted butter, softened

1 large egg yolk

Makes about 30 cookies

Cinnamon Sugar Cookies

1 1/4 cups flour

1 cup sugar

2 teaspoons cinnamon

1 teaspoon baking powder

1/4 teaspoon salt

1/3 cup chopped walnuts or pecans

1/4 to 1/2 cup sugar for rolling cookies

4 ounces (1 stick) unsalted butter

1 beaten egg

1 teaspoon vanilla

Preheat oven to 375 degrees.

Cream the butter with the one cup of sugar. Add the egg and vanilla; mix well.

Sift together the flour, cinnamon, baking powder, and salt. Stir in the nuts and mix well. Now stir this into the butter mixture.

Roll the dough into 1-inch balls. Roll these in the remaining sugar. Flatten slightly with the bottom of a glass.

Bake on ungreased cookie sheets for 10-12 minutes. Cool on wire racks. Store in tins.

Makes 3 dozen cookies

Coconut-Cranberry Cookies

In a large bowl, with a mixer on medium speed, beat 1 1/2 cups butter, sugar, orange peel, and vanilla until smooth.

In a medium bowl, mix flour, baking powder, and salt. Add to butter mixture, stir to mix, then beat on low speed until dough comes together, about 5 minutes or longer if necessary for smoothness. Mix in cranberries and coconut.

Shape dough into 1-inch balls and place about 2 inches apart on buttered 12 by 15-inch baking sheets.

Bake in a 350 degree oven until cookie edges just begin to brown, 8 to 11 minutes (shorter baking time will yield a chewier cookie; longer baking time will yield a crispier cookie). If baking two sheets at once in one oven, switch their positions halfway through baking. Let cookies cool on sheets for 5 minutes, then use a wide spatula to transfer to racks to cool completely.

2 cups sugar

1 tablespoon grated orange peel

3 1/2 cups flour

1 teaspoon baking powder

1/4 teaspoon salt

1 1/2 cups dried cranberries

1 1/2 cups sweetened flaked dried coconut

1 1/2 cups butter at room temperature

2 teaspoons vanilla

Makes about 6 dozen cookies

Coconut Garden Cookies

Preheat oven to 300 degrees. Cream the butter with the sugar. Sift together the flour and salt. Stir in the coconut. Mix into the butter mixture; blend well. Shape into rolls and wrap in wax paper. Refrigerate until firm. Cut into 1/4-inch slices. Bake for 20 minutes or until lightly browned.

2 cups flour

1 cup sugar

1 teaspoon salt

8 ounces (2 sticks) unsalted butter

1 1/2 cups coconut

Makes 3 dozen cookies

offee Bars

1 1/2 cups sifted flour

1/2 teaspoon baking
   powder

1/2 teaspoon baking
   soda

1/2 teaspoon salt

1/2 teaspoon cinnamon

1/2 cup white sugar

1/2 cup brown sugar

1/4 cup shortening

1 egg

1/2 cup hot coffee

1/2 cup raisins

1/4 cup pecans or
   walnuts, finely
   chopped

ICING

1 tablespoon hot coffee

2 tablespoons butter

1 1/2 cups powdered
   sugar

Preheat oven to 350 degrees.

Sift flour, baking powder, salt, cinnamon and soda together. In separate bowl, cream shortening and sugar together; add eggs and beat well. Add hot coffee and blend. Add flour mixture, raisins and nuts.

Spread in a greased 10x13 inch pan. Bake for 15-20 minutes.

COFFEE ICING

Melt butter in hot coffee. Add powdered sugar until spreading consistency. Ice bars while still warm.

Coffee Cake

Preheat oven to 350 degrees. Grease and flour a 10-inch tube pan or Bundt pan.

Put the butter in a large mixing bowl and beat for several seconds. Add the sugar and beat until smooth. Add the eggs and beat for 2 minutes, or until light and creamy. Put the flour, baking powder, baking soda, and salt in a bowl and stir with a fork to blend well. Add the flour mixture to the butter mixture and beat until smooth. Add the sour cream and mix well.

Spoon the batter into the pan. Bake for about 50 minutes or until a toothpick comes out clean when inserted into the center. Remove from the oven and let rest for 5 minutes in the pan. Invert onto a rack and cool a little bit before slicing. Serve warm.

1 cup sugar

2 1/2 cups flour

2 teaspoons baking powder

1 teaspoon baking soda

1 teaspoon salt

2 sticks butter, room temperature

3 eggs

1 cup sour cream

Cowboy Cookies

2 cups wheat pastry
  flour

2 cups rolled oats

1 teaspoon baking soda

1/2 teaspoon salt

3/4 cup brown sugar

3/4 cup sugar

1 package chocolate
  chips

1 cup nuts

2 eggs

1 cup oil

1 teaspoon vanilla

Mix first six dry ingredients together.

Then add eggs, oil, and vanilla, mix well.

Add chocolate chips and nuts.

Form into balls.

Bake at 350 degrees for 15-20 minutes.

How these cookies got their name, I'm not quite sure. This is my mother's recipe; it's simple and produces great cookies. A favorite for four generations.

Makes about 6 dozen cookies

rème Brulee

Preheat oven to 275 degrees.

In a small pan, bring cream, 2 tablespoons sugar, vanilla bean, and salt just to a boil over medium heat. Remove from heat and set aside to cool. Remove and discard vanilla bean.

In another bowl, whisk egg yolks with 1 tablespoon of sugar until sugar dissolves. Slowly whisk in cooled cream (if it is not cool, yolk will scramble). Strain through a fine sieve.

Divide custard mixture between 4 shallow gratin dishes (each about 1/2 cup in capacity). Place dishes in a baking pan, then place pan in oven. Pour enough cold water into pan to come about halfway up sides of dishes. Bake until custards set, 30-35 minutes. Remove from heat; let cool.

Cover cooled custards with plastic wrap. Chill in refrigerator for at least 4 hours or overnight. Before serving, sprinkle 1 1/2 teaspoons sugar on each custard and use a small blowtorch to carmelize tops, holding torch at an angle (flame should barely touch surface) to brown sugar.

5 tablespoons sugar

Small pinch salt

2 cups heavy cream

4 egg yolks

1/2 vanilla bean, split

Serves 4

$\mathscr{E}$spresso Brittle

1/3 cup espresso beans

1 1/2 cups sugar

3/4 cup light corn syrup

1/2 cup water

**3 tablespoons unsalted
butter, cut into pieces**

Preheat oven to 350 degrees.

Place the espresso beans on a baking sheet and toast them for 8-10 minutes (or use pre-roasted beans instead). Let cool, crack by placing them in a plastic bag and hitting with a mallet. Cover a 10x15-inch jelly roll pan with aluminum foil and lightly oil the foil. Spread the cracked espresso beans evenly over the foil.

In a medium-sized, heavy saucepan, combine the sugar, syrup, water and bring the mixture to a boil, stirring until the sugar dissolves. Continue to boil until the liquid becomes amber in color. Remove from heat, stir in the butter, and pour the mixture evenly over the beans. Spread the mixture evenly while still warm. Let cool, then break into irregular pieces.

Makes about 1 pound

Flaky Cinnamon Twists

Preheat the oven to 375 degrees. Dissolve yeast in the warm water and sugar. Let stand until bubbly. Combine flour, shortening, and salt until crumbly.

Whip the eggs. Beat in the sour cream, vanilla, and yeast mixture. Add to the dry ingredients and blend. Refrigerate for 2 hours.

Sprinkle the sugar onto a board. Turn out the dough onto the sugar. Sprinkle more sugar over the dough and roll to a 12-inch square. Fold dough to center from either side. Roll again, sprinkling with sugar. Repeat the folding and rolling process 4 times, adding as much sugar as necessary to prevent sticking.

Cut dough into 1-inch by 4-inch strips. Sprinkle with more sugar and some cinnamon. Twist loosely. Place on an ungreased baking sheet. Bake for 20 minutes, or until nicely browned.

4 cups flour

1 package dry yeast

1 teaspoon sugar

2 cups sugar

1/2 teaspoon salt

Cinnamon

1/2 cup warm water

1 cup vegetable shortening

3 eggs

1 cup sour cream

1 teaspoon vanilla

Makes 36

Gloria's Classic Shortbread

1/4 cup confectioners' sugar (powdered)

3/4 cup all-purpose flour

1/4 cup rice flour (if rice flour is difficult to find, substitute with all-purpose flour)

1/8 teaspoon baking powder

1/8 teaspoon salt

1 stick of butter

1/2 teaspoon vanilla

Preheat oven to 375 degrees.

Cream the butter with confectioners' sugar, add the vanilla. Sift all-purpose flour, rice flour, baking powder, and salt: add to cream mixture.

Pat the dough into an 8-inch circle or 8-inch square on an ungreased cookie sheet. This recipe gives you a very soft, delicate dough — so be patient with it. Before baking, score the dough —making 6 wedges, and mark the edge with the tines of a fork.

Bake the shortbread for about 20 minutes, or until the edge is golden brown.

While the shortbread is still warm, cut it into the wedges with a sharp knife.

Try adding some chopped rosemary to the dough for a new twist on this classic recipe.

Hot Mocha Sauce

In a saucepan, melt the butter and chocolate. Stir in the coffee, corn syrup, sugar, and salt. Bring the mixture to a boil. Boil the sauce gently, without stirring, until thick and smooth — about 10 minutes. Stir in vanilla. Serve hot.

1 cup sugar

3 ounces unsweetened chocolate

Pinch of salt

3 tablespoons unsalted butter

1/4 cup light corn syrup

1 teaspoon vanilla

1/2 cup strong coffee

Makes 1 cup

Lemon Pound Cake

1 2/3 cups sugar

2 cups cake flour

1/2 teaspoon salt

2 teaspoons grated
lemon peel

2 sticks butter

5 eggs

Preheat oven to 325 degrees. Grease and flour one 9 x 5 x 3-inch loaf pan.

Put the butter in a large mixing bowl and beat until creamy. Slowly add the sugar, beating constantly, until the mixture is well blended. Add the eggs, one at a time, beating well after each addition. Add the flour and salt and beat until smooth and thoroughly blended. Add the lemon peel and beat another few seconds.

Pour the batter into the pan and smooth the top with a spatula. Bake for about an hour, or until a straw comes out clean when inserted into the center. Let cool in the pan 5 minutes before turning onto a rack to cool completely.

Mocha Truffle Cake

Preheat oven to 350 degrees.

Completely line the bottom and sides of a 10-inch cake pan with foil, allowing some of the foil to extend beyond the top of the pan. Smooth out the foil as much as possible. Generously coat with some of the butter.

Melt the chocolate with the remaining butter, coffee, and sugar over low heat. Simmer over low heat until the sugar dissolves.

Beat the eggs until thick, about 5 minutes. Stir into the chocolate mixture. Pour into the prepared pan. Bake for approximately 50 minutes, or until the center is just set. Cool completely in the pan. Cover and refrigerate in the pan until firm, at least 8 hours or overnight.

FROSTING

A few hours prior to serving, whip the cream with the sugar and vanilla. Invert the cake onto a serving platter. Carefully remove the foil. Frost the cake with the whipped cream. Garnish with the Chocolate Flakes. To make Chocolate Flakes, melt semisweet chocolate and spread on a marble slab or large flat plate. Let the chocolate harden. Scrape against it with a knife and it will flake into thin pieces.

1 pound (4 sticks) unsalted butter, cut into pieces

1 pound semisweet chocolate

2 cups sugar

1 cup strong coffee

8 large eggs, room temperature

FROSTING

1/4 cup powdered sugar

1 cup heavy cream

1/4 teaspoon vanilla

Chocolate Flakes

Serves 10-12

Mother's Cookies

3/4 cup sugar

1/2 teaspoon baking soda

1/2 teaspoon salt

1 teaspoon cinnamon

3/4 cup flour

1/2 cup rolled oats

1 cup cornflakes or Wheaties

1/2 cup shortening

1 egg

3/4 cup golden raisins

Preheat oven to 350 degrees. Don't grease the baking sheet(s).

Put the shortening, sugar, and egg in a mixing bowl. Beat until smooth. Add the baking soda, salt, cinnamon, and flour and beat until well blended. Add the oats, cornflakes or Wheaties, and raisins. This is going to be a stiff dough, but exert a little vigor and stir until the oats, flakes, and raisins are well distributed.

Drop rounded tablespoons of dough onto the baking sheet(s) about 1 inch apart. Bake 15 to 17 minutes, or until lightly golden.

Remove from the oven and let cool.

Makes about 3 dozen cookies

Old Fashioned Crumb Cake

Preheat oven to 350 degrees. Sift together the flour, 3/4 teaspoon of the cinnamon, and salt. Add both sugars and the oil. Mix until fluffy. Measure out 3/4 cup of this mix for the topping: add the nuts, the remaining 1 teaspoon of cinnamon, and nutmeg. Place to the side. To the remaining flour mixture, add the baking powder, baking soda, egg, and buttermilk. Stir until smooth. Spoon into a well-greased 9x13-inch pan and smooth the top. Sprinkle with the topping mixture and press in lightly with the back of a spoon. Bake for 30 to 35 minutes, or until a tester inserted in the center comes out clean.

2 1/4 cups sifted flour

1 3/4 teaspoons cinnamon

1/4 teaspoon salt

1 cup packed brown sugar

3/4 cup sugar

1 teaspoon baking powder

1/2 teaspoon baking soda

1/2 teaspoon nutmeg

1/2 cup chopped nuts

3/4 cup vegetable oil

1 egg, lightly beaten

1 cup buttermilk

Serves 8

Orange Chocolate Chip Cookies

2 cups flour

1/2 cup whole-wheat flour

1 teaspoon baking soda

1 teaspoon salt

1 cup sugar

1 cup packed brown sugar

1/2 cup (1 stick) softened butter

1/2 cup chopped walnuts

1 cup semisweet chocolate chips

Grated peel of 1 orange

2 tablespoons oil

2 eggs

Preheat oven to 350 degrees.

Line a baking sheet with bakers' parchment.

Cream together the sugars, butter, oil and grated orange peel. Add the eggs and mix well.

Combine the flours, soda and salt: stir to mix. Add to the creamed mixture and blend well. Stir in the nuts and chocolate chips. Drop by the tablespoonful or scoop onto the baking sheet; flatten slightly to make thick, round disc shapes. Allow about 3 inches between each cookie.

Bake for 10 minutes, or until the cookies are light brown. Let cool on the sheet a few minutes before transferring the cookies to a rack to cool completely.

Makes about 2 1/2 dozen cookies

Poppy Seed Cake

Preheat oven to 350 degrees.

Combine poppy seeds and buttermilk.

Cream butter and the one cup of sugar until light. Beat in eggs, one at a time.

Sift the flour with the baking powder, baking soda, and salt. Blend into the egg mixture and add vanilla and orange peel. Stir in poppy seeds and buttermilk.

Pour half of the batter into a buttered 6-8 cup Bundt pan. Sprinkle with the sugar and cinnamon. Cover with the remaining batter. Bake for approximately 50-55 minutes, or until a tester inserted in the center comes out clean.

Let stand for 15 minutes. Invert and cool on a rack.

2 1/2 cups sifted flour

2 teaspoons baking powder

1 teaspoon baking soda

2 tablespoons sugar

1 cup sugar

1/2 teaspoon salt

1 teaspoon cinnamon

1/2 cup poppy seeds

1 1/2 tablespoons grated orange peel

8 ounces (2 sticks) unsalted butter

4 eggs

1 cup buttermilk

1 teaspoon vanilla

Serves 8-10

Special K Cookies

Preheat oven to 350 degrees.

In a mixer or with electric beaters, cream the butter and sugar until fluffy. Beat in the vanilla and set aside.

In a separate bowl, sift together the flour and baking powder. Stir the flour mixture into the butter mixture until thoroughly blended. Gently stir in the cereal. Drop the dough by teaspoons onto a baking sheet, allowing a few inches between them. Bake until lightly browned around the edges, 10 to 13 minutes. Let the cookies sit on the baking sheet for a minute or two before transferring them to a cake rack to cool. Continue baking the remaining dough in batches.

1 cup sugar

1 1/2 cups flour

1 1/2 teaspoons baking powder

2 cups Special K cereal

1 cup unsalted butter

1 teaspoon vanilla

Makes about 4 dozen cookies

Stove-top Peanut Brittle

2 cups sugar

1/2 teaspoon salt

2 teaspoons baking soda

3 cups raw peanuts, skins on

1 cup light corn syrup

2 tablespoons butter

1/2 cup water

In a heavy saucepan, heat sugar, corn syrup, water and salt to a rolling boil. Add peanuts. Reduce heat to medium and stir constantly. Cook until the syrup spins a thread (293 degrees on candy thermometer). This will take about 45 minutes.

Add butter, then baking soda. Beat rapidly and pour on a buttered surface, spreading to 1/4-inch thickness. When cool, break into pieces. Store in an airtight container.

Makes 3 1/2 pounds of candy

Tosca Cake

Preheat oven to 375 degrees. Beat eggs and sugar together. Stir in flour, vanilla, and melted butter. Pour into a greased and floured 9-inch square pan. Bake for 20 minutes. Spread topping across the top of the cake. Continue baking for 10 minutes, or until tester inserted in the center comes out clean.

TOPPING

In a small saucepan, combine all the topping ingredients. Heat but do not allow to come to a boil.

CAKE

3/4 cup sugar

1 cup flour

2 eggs

2 teaspoons vanilla

4 ounces unsalted butter, melted

TOPPING

1/2 cup sliced almonds

1/2 cup sugar

3 tablespoons flour

6 tablespoons unsalted butter

2 tablespoons half and half

Serves 6 - 8